WASHED OUT BRIDGES AND OTHER DISASTERS

Recent Doonesbury Books by G.B. Trudeau

Read My Lips, Make My Day, Eat Quiche and Die!
Give Those Nymphs Some Hooters!
You're Smokin' Now, Mr. Butts!
I'd Go With the Helmet, Ray
Welcome to Club Scud!
What Is It, Tink, Is Pan in Trouble?
Quality Time on Highway 1

In Large Format

The Doonesbury Chronicles
Doonesbury's Greatest Hits
The People's Doonesbury
Doonesbury Dossier: The Reagan Years
Doonesbury Deluxe: Selected Glances Askance
Recycled Doonesbury: Second Thoughts on a Gilded Age
Action Figure!
The Portable Doonesbury

A DOONESBURY BOOK
by G. B. TRUDEAU

WASHED OUT BRIDGES AND OTHER DISASTERS

ANDREWS and McMEEL   A UNIVERSAL PRESS SYNDICATE COMPANY   KANSAS CITY

——————————— ATTENTION: SCHOOLS AND BUSINESSES ———————————

Andrews and McMeel books are available at quantity discounts with bulk purchase for educational, business,
or sales promotional use. For information, please write to: Special Sales Department, Andrews and McMeel,
4900 Main Street, Kansas City, Missouri 64112.

"To my wife, this is *Moby Dick*."

— COLUMNIST KEVIN COWHERD, ON *BRIDGES*

18

Panel 1: HEY, **KIDS OF ALL AGES!** STILL DISAPPOINTED YOU MISSED ROSS PEROT'S MAIL-IN POLL IN "T.V. GUIDE"? WISH **YOU** HAD A WAY TO WEIGH IN ON THE BIG ISSUES?

Panel 2: WELL, GOOD NEWS, CAMPERS—NOW YOU **DO!** WELCOME TO OUR FIRST ANNUAL **CARTOON TOWN MEETING!** JUST FILL IN THE ATTACHED POLL, AND YOU, TOO, CAN BE PART OF THE NEW DEMOCRACY! ALL QUESTIONS **GUARANTEED** AS UNBIASED AS MR. PEROT'S!

THE FIRST ANNUAL
CARTOON TOWN MEETING

Please check off the appropriate boxes.

1. Do you think the White House should continue to kowtow to a third-place, on-again, off-again, presidential wannabe?

   No ☐   Yes ☐   Not sure ☐

2. Do you think Congress should listen to lectures about "special interests" from someone who was once the U.S.'s largest individual contributor to politicians, 12 of whom later voted to give him a special $15 million tax break?

   No ☐   Yes ☐   Not sure ☐

3. Do you think anyone should listen to a egomaniacal, bigoted conspiracy-theorist capable of investigating not only his enemies, but his own supporters and family?

   No ☐   Yes ☐   Not sure ☐

Send to: Cartoon Town Meeting, c/o UNIVERSAL PRESS SYNDICATE
4900 MAIN STREET, KANSAS CITY, MO 64112

WE'LL BE PRINTING THE POLL RESULTS IN THIS SPACE NEXT MONTH, SO **ACT NOW!** LET YOUR GOVERNMENT KNOW HOW **YOU** FEEL ON THESE IMPORTANT NATIONAL ISSUES!

GBTrudeau

22

25

28

30

41

50

51

Panel 1: THE CONTESSA HAS A CHANGE OF HEART...
WHAT I DID WAS FOR LOVE, MIKE. I CANNOT ACCEPT YOUR MONEY. INVEST IN AMERICA.
OKAY.

Panel 2: AND SO HE DID.
HEY, MAN, HAVE YOU **REALLY** PUT HUNDREDS OF INNER CITY KIDS THROUGH MED SCHOOL?
NO BIG DEAL.

Panel 3: NO BIG DEAL? MAN, YOU'RE SPENDIN' YOUR LIFE HELPIN' HOMIES OUTA THE HOOD, WHEN YOU COULD BE SITTIN' IN A POOL UP IN SANTA BARBARA!
GOOD POINT.

Panel 4: CLOSURE.
SO HOW'VE YOU BEEN, CONTESSA?
GRAVELY ILL. MY LIFE WAS SAVED BY A BRILLIANT, YOUNG BLACK SURGEON.
©B Trudeau

Panel 5: MIKE'S SUMMER FANTASY HAS HIM POWER-BREAKFASTING AT L.A.'S FOUR SEASONS HOTEL.
...AND I SEE MICHAEL DOUGLAS PLAYING ME!

Panel 6: SUDDENLY...
HI.
GOOD LORD! IT'S... IT'S **SHARON STONE!**

Panel 7: I SAW YOU ACROSS THE ROOM. I WANT YOU. NOW.
NOW?
CALL FOR YOU, MR. DOONESBURY!

Panel 8: MIKE? BILL CLINTON! YOUR COUNTRY NEEDS YOU! NOW!
UH... NOW?
©B Trudeau

Panel 9: MIKE BLOWS OFF SHARON STONE...
LATER, BABY! DUTY CALLS!

Panel 10: A FEW HOURS LATER...
MIKE, HERE'S THE SITUATION: AZERBAIDZHAN IS ABOUT TO BLOW, THREATENING ALL OUR INTERESTS IN THE REGION!

Panel 11: YOU'RE OUR LEADING EXPERT ON AZERBAIDZHAN! **WHAT** SHOULD WE DO?
UM...
PHONE CALL, MR. DOONESBURY!

Panel 12: MIKE, IS THIS ALMOST OVER? DINNER'S READY.
UM... IN A MINUTE. WHERE'S AZERBAIDZHAN?
©B Trudeau

69

90